shadow work

WORKBOOK

DANIELLE MASSI, LMFT

STERLING ETHOS
New York

STERLING ETHOS
New York

STERLING ETHOS and the distinctive Sterling Ethos logo are registered trademarks of Sterling Publishing Co., Inc.

Text © 2025 Danielle Massi
Art © 2025 Union Square & Co., LLC

All rights reserved. No part of this publication may be reproduced, stored in a retrieval system, or transmitted in any form or by any means (including electronic, mechanical, photocopying, recording, or otherwise) without prior written permission from the publisher.

This publication is a component of *The Shadow Work Deck* (ISBN: 978-1-4549-6023-2) and is not to be sold separately.

For information about custom editions, special sales, and premium purchases, please contact specialsales@unionsquareandco.com.

Manufactured in China

2 4 6 8 10 9 7 5 3 1

unionsquareandco.com

Cover and interior design by Stacy Wakefield Forte
Cover and interior art by Inktally
Images on pages 44–45 by Pham Thanh Loc/ The Noun Project

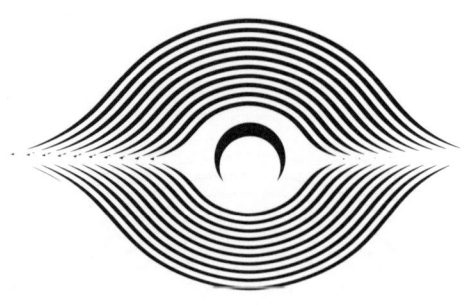

welcome to the shadow workbook...

Taking the next step in investigating your shadow is a courageous decision. This workbook is intended to be used with *The Shadow Work Deck,* as an additional tool in your exploration. The themes in this workbook align with the suits in the deck, offering you the opportunity to venture a bit deeper into the topics that your card pulls are nudging you toward.

USING THE WORKBOOK

The workbook can be used in two ways: with the cards in *The Shadow Work Deck,* or on its own.

IF YOU ARE USING THE WORKBOOK WITH THE CARDS:

Before you begin working with the prompts and exercises in these pages, pull cards from *The Shadow Work Deck.* Your card pulls will guide where your energy should go and the topics you can explore with greater depth. Flip to the workbook pages that coincide with the cards you have pulled, and complete the corresponding exercises.

IF YOU ARE USING THE WORKBOOK ON ITS OWN:

Take a few deep breaths to center your body and ground yourself in the present. Let your intuition be your guide as you work through the prompts that call to you, or let yourself flip to a random page.

inner child exercises

1. KEEP YOUR INNER CHILD SAFE
Create boundaries and healing opportunities

Think back to a moment in your childhood that made a long-lasting impact on you because you needed a level of safety that wasn't there. Think about who should have been there protecting you, and why they might not have done so.

What would you tell your inner child in this moment if you were the adult? Write it below.

....

....

....

....

....

Now turn that statement into a mantra for yourself. For example, if you wrote above that you would tell your inner child that although this moment is scary, this moment will pass, your mantra could be the following: Although this moment is scary, this moment will pass.

Your Mantra:

....

....

....

....

Take this mantra and recite it to yourself whenever you are feeling triggered by feelings of instability or a lack of grounding and safety.

2. CHILDLIKE WONDERS
Embrace freedom and play

Circle options from this list that you would like to try, and create a plan for doing them!

Play on a playground

Bird-watch

Draw with chalk

Watch a movie from your childhood

Ride a bike

Go for a walk with a friend

Finger paint

Eat a meal you enjoyed as a kid

Daydream

Visit a petting zoo

Roller-skate

Dance/sing to music from your childhood

Play with chalk

Read a favorite book from your childhood

How and when will you do this activity?

3. OLD WOUNDS
Repeating themes from childhood

What is a repeating theme from your childhood?

....

....

When you experienced it before, how was it handled?

....

....

What can be done differently this time to break this pattern and stop it from ever showing up again?

....

....

ancestral healing exercises

1. GENERATIONAL CURSES
Witness the patterns

What patterns do you experience within your family in each of these categories, and with whom?

Negative Behaviors	Psychological/ Physiological Ailments	Persistent Life Challenges

2. FAMILY LINEAGE
Reconnect with your ancestors

Your ancestors are always connecting with you, but you may not have noticed their gentle nudges before. When they are looking to connect, they will send you a symbol, like a feather, a dime, repeating number sequences like 11:11 or 333, etc. If you know what the symbols are, fill them in below. If you have not noticed any symbols before, you can choose the symbols you would like to receive and write them below.

Symbols from your ancestors:

....

....

....

....

....

3. REWRITE THE STORY
Begin a new chapter

Take a story that your family has clung to and perpetuated, and craft a reframed version of it that better suits your new personal narrative.

past life exercises

1. PAST LIFE POWER
Own your gifts

gratitude list

Make a list of three moments from your past, and write why you are grateful for them!

1.

2.

3.

2. SOUL JOURNEY
Discover where your soul has been

Explore these prompts to uncover where your soul has been.

1. Did you have a favorite subject in history class that was uniquely interesting to you?

....

....

....

2. Have you ever experienced déjà vu or felt like you actually remember a historical person, place, or period of time?

....

....

....

3. Do you have a talent or a fear that does not have origins that you can explain?

4. Do you have a recurring dream that feels more like a memory than a dream?

3. SCARS OF THE PAST
Understanding hidden triggers

Close your eyes, and ask yourself out loud, "What is the hidden trigger that my soul is asking me to recognize?" When the answer comes forth, write it here:

Think about how that particular pain point has appeared in different areas of your life. Then close your eyes once more and ask yourself, "What is this hidden trigger trying to show me about myself?" Write that answer here:

....

....

....

....

....

....

Allow that answer to settle deep within, illuminating not only the scar but also why it has been ever-present.

womb work exercises

1. DIVINE FEMININE
Creativity, freedom, and flow

Tap into your creativity and flow! Color this page while focusing on the process, not the outcome.

2. LET IT GO
Release your attachment to the trauma you carry

Think of one of the hardest moments in your life that you can consciously remember.

Name it:
....

....

What did this moment teach you about yourself?

....

....

....

....

....

How has this moment altered your behavior?

....

....

....

....

What would releasing your attachment to this moment mean for you and for your life?

....

....

....

....

3. RETHINK YOUR RELATIONSHIPS
Who are you holding onto that you shouldn't be?

What relationships in your life might you be holding onto that you shouldn't? List them below, and write why you've outgrown them in the box beneath.

Name:

Name:

Name:

Name:

Name:

Finally, if you were to release your attachments to these relationships, how might you change?

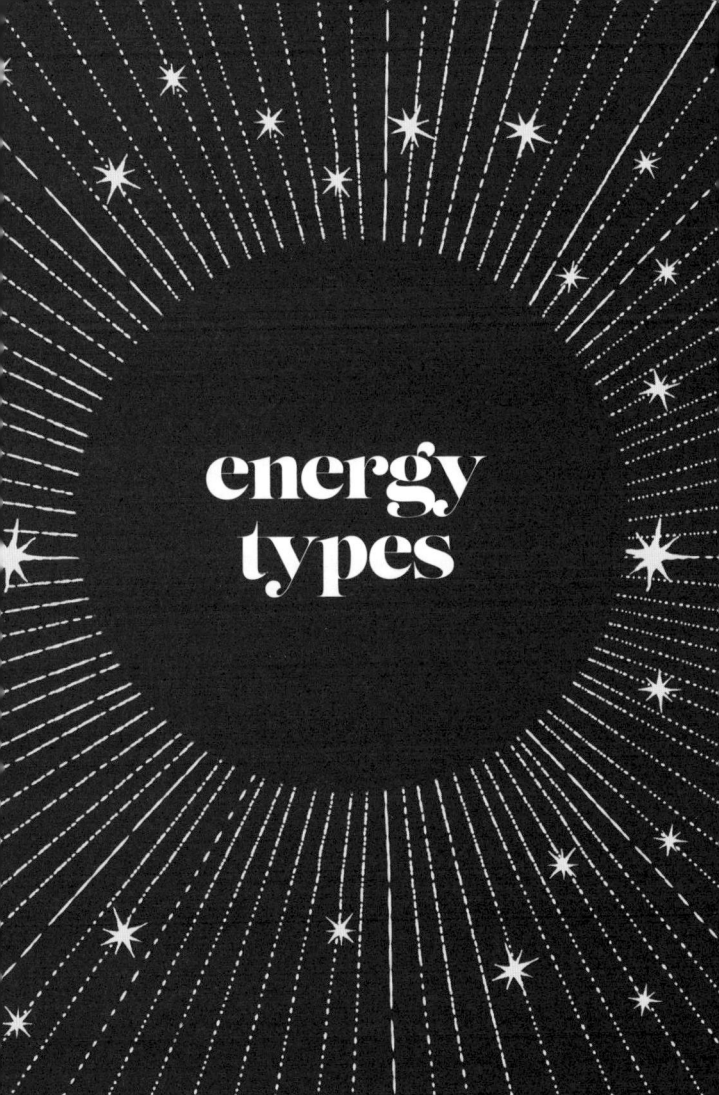

chakra exercises

1. ROOTED
Ground your energy

Close your eyes, and take a deep breath in through the nose and out through the mouth. Then bring all your attention to the base of your spine. As you focus on this chakra and continue to breathe deeply, imagine a red wheel spinning away anything that is throwing off your alignment. Visualize the wheel releasing this stuck, stagnant energy until you feel totally in balance. Then open your eyes and create a visual representation of your wheel here:

2. OPEN YOUR CROWN
Connect with divine guidance and wisdom

Spend two to three minutes imagining the fog within your mind clearing, like the sun emerging after a rainstorm. As you create this visualization for yourself, breathe deeply, with your inhale bringing in the sun and your exhale clearing the fog of your mind.

When this is completed, ask yourself the following yes or no questions, and feel the answers coming from the Universe, down into your body through your crown chakra.

1. Do I receive guidance from my spirit guides?
   YES ☐ **NO** ☐

2. Am I ready to let my spirit guides help me?
   YES ☐ **NO** ☐

3. Is there more shadow work that must be done before I can feel my crown chakra open fully?
   YES ☐ **NO** ☐

If the answer to the last question is yes, pull a card from *The Shadow Work Deck* to discover what type of shadow work is needed.

3. AJNA
Open your third eye

release fear and doubt

Use this activity to help plan how you will release the denser emotions that block your third eye.

What am I afraid of?

[   ]

How has that fear protected me?

....

....

My plan for releasing that fear:

[   ]

Why do I doubt myself?

How has doubt protected me?

My plan for releasing doubt:

4. MANIPURA
Take control of your life

You already have all the answers! Your body knows what to do. Use the Human Pendulum Technique (you can read more about it in my book, *Shadow Work*). The basics are below:

Begin by drinking a large glass of water to fully hydrate the body. Don't skip this step; the water in your body is what enables the human pendulum to move, so you need to be properly hydrated for this task.

In a moment, you will begin asking yes or no questions out loud and noticing how your body reacts. Your body will move in one of four directions: forward, back, left, or right. Every person is different, so you will need to discover in which direction your body moves for yes and which for no.

Stand with your feet hip-width apart and keep your hands down at your sides. Calibrate your human pendulum by asking the following questions that you know the answers to:

1. Is my name _____?
   (e.g., Is my name Danielle?)
   Notice in which direction you move for yes.

2. Is my name Mother Goose?
   Notice in which direction you move for no.

3. Am I currently living in_____?
   Notice in which direction you move for yes.

4. Am I currently living on Mars?
   Notice in which direction you move for no.

Now that you have your human pendulum calibrated, feel free to ask yourself any question that you desire a yes or no answer to, and see which way your body moves after you ask. With this technique, you'll receive definitive answers that you can trust because they come from your body's own inner wisdom.

5. VISHUDDHA
Use your voice

Write down what you truly wish you could say if there was nothing holding you back, then read it out loud to yourself in the mirror every day this week.

6. ANAHATA
Where has your heart been closed off?

Make the bold choice to open your heart to new possibilities. Think of five situations where you have responded with a closed heart in the past, then write how you will respond going forward.

Then	Now
1.	1.
2.	2.
3.	3.
4.	4.
5.	5.

7. SACRAL WOUNDS
Heal your connection to your sensuality

What is your connection to your sensuality?

....

....

....

....

How do you feel in your naval center?

....

....

....

....

And what shadow could potentially be slowing your energy center down?

....

....

....

....

8. EXPAND YOUR AURA
Become the master of your energy

Describe three areas where you recognize that you may be more powerful than you have let yourself believe.

1.

2.

3.

How does seeing these written down make you feel?

archetype exercises

1. THE PERSONA
Recognize the different masks you wear

Give a name to each of the masks you wear, decorate and color them based on your own visual representation of them, and write their characteristics next to them.

Name:

Characteristics:

Name:

Characteristics:

Name:

Characteristics:

2. THE HERO'S JOURNEY
Transformation and adventure

Where are you being called to push the boundaries of your life and step boldly into the unknown? It might be an opportunity at work, a new relationship, a journey of self-discovery, or something else entirely.

....

....

....

What hesitations do you have about this journey?

....

....

....

Why will you commit to it anyway? Create a convincing argument.

3. THE MOTHER
Nurturing and protection

What can you do now to let yourself replenish? Circle any of these that you would like to try, and decide on a plan for doing them.

Cleansing bath

Morning meditation

Reiki healing

Massage

Breath work

Moon rituals

Gardening

....

....

....

....

....

4. THE SHADOW
What are you repressing?

Pick a moment from your past that haunts you. What is it?

....

What emotion is most tied to that moment?

    Fear   *Doubt*

    Guilt   *Jealousy*

    Shame   *Anger*

    Exhaustion   *Other:* _____

When does that emotion show up for you in your daily life?

....

....

....

astrology exercises

1. DARK MOON
Ending of a cycle. Opportunity for integration

journal prompts for the dark moon:

1. How do I resist taking pauses in my life?

2. What lessons do I believe the Universe has been trying to teach me in recent weeks?

....

....

....

....

3. How can I slow down to fully integrate what I've learned?

....

....

....

....

....

2. NEW MOON
Get clear on your intentions

intention-setting meditation exercise

Take a moment to become present with your body, doing a scan from the crown of your head down to the soles of your feet. Breathe deeply, in through your nose and out through your mouth. Place your left hand on your heart, and your right hand on your belly. As you continue to breathe with your hands in this position, visualize how you want your journey to end. Where do you wish to be at its completion? What do you hope to experience on your journey? And how do you hope to feel when you reach the end?

Pick three feelings you hope to feel when this is over, or add your own below:

Grateful   *Accomplished*

Elated   *Validated*

Relieved   *Motivated*

Overjoyed   *Peaceful*

Inspired   *Other:*

Thrilled   _____

Write your three chosen feelings below:

1. _____

2. _____

3. _____

3. FULL MOON
Reap what you have sown

Write a letter to yourself as if you are writing to another person. Note all the work you have done and all your accomplishments, and give yourself praise for your continuous effort. When you are done, read the letter as if someone else wrote it for you.

For instance, you might write the following:

"Dear me,

I am so proud of everything you have accomplished this year. Last year was a low point, and you made the bold decision to crawl out of the depths of that darkness and soar to new heights . . ."

Dear   ,

4. CHIRON
Transmute your pain into power

In the outer circle, write your deepest pains. In the inner circle, write the strength that this pain has given you.

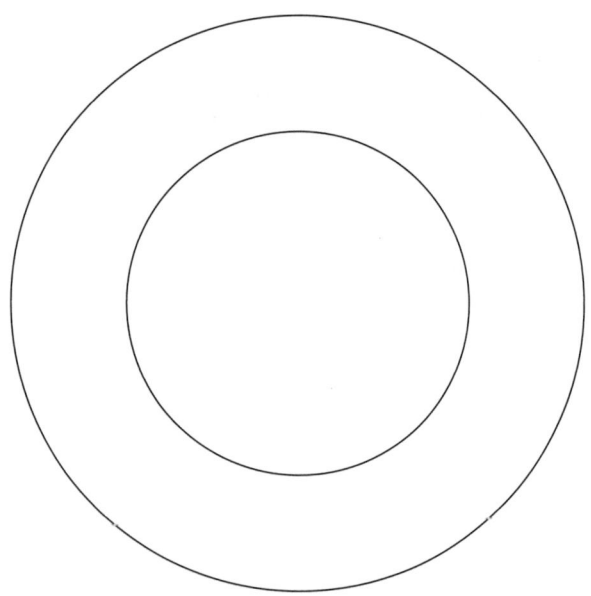

5. BLACK MOON LILITH
Harness your power

If you are honest with yourself, what things are true to your deepest, most primal nature? List them unabashedly below.

_____

_____

_____

_____

_____

_____

_____

6. MERCURY RETROGRADE
Learn to communicate

Get clear about what you want. Write short, concise sentences that convey exactly what you desire right now.

1.

2.

3.

4.

activation exercises

1. THE EGO
Overcoming your inner critic

The little voice in your head is holding you back!

Where does this particular voice come from?

Think about who the voice sounds like. Maybe they are phrases that a parent, teacher, mentor, old relationship, grandparent, or coach has used with you in the past.

Name the voice:

....

What phrases is the inner critic voice using to hold you back?

That inner critic is *wrong*! Provide evidence to argue against the voice:

....

....

....

....

....

....

....

The next time your inner critic gets loud, name it and argue against it. Then use your intuition to make your decisions instead.

2. KARMIC LOOPS
Break the chain

Accepting the role of cycle breaker can feel like a heavy and isolating burden. Use this page to reflect on everything that comes up for you as you accept this task.

3. SACRED RAGE
Unleash your anger to amplify your power

What are you enraged about right now? Let your anger *flow* out of your body and onto the page.

_____

_____

_____

_____

_____

_____

Tear this page out and burn your anger away!

4. STARSEED ENERGY
Connect with galactic groups

Try these practices to connect with galactic groups. Circle one to begin with, then reflect on your experience.

Meditation

Journaling

Nature walks

Stargazing

Learning about astrology

Reflection:

5. DARK GODDESS
Embrace the darker path: intuition, mystery, and magic

Relinquishing control to the Dark Goddess often means being led to explore new magical pathways. How can this moment of profound heaviness lead you to embrace intuition, mystery, and magic?

6. LIFE LENS
Understand how you see the world

discover your life lens—exercise from *shadow work* by danielle massi

Which feels most important to you?

1. Creating a life of freedom, where you can choose to live on your own terms.
2. Having control over your life; feeling like you are in the driver's seat at all times.
3. Making sure that things are fair and equitable for you and those around you.
4. Feeling powerful in your life and career choices.
5. Needing to feel safe and secure in your life and in your body.

Which of these would make you feel the worst?

1. Being stuck in a career path that doesn't fulfill you or allow you to pursue hobbies.
2. Someone trying to tell you how to do something or how to live your life.
3. Witnessing injustices against yourself or others and not being able to do anything about it.
4. Watching others rise above you as you remain stuck behind.
5. Feeling helpless or hopeless in your life or your body.

Your Life Lens based on your answers:

1: Freedom
2: Control
3: Fairness
4: Power
5: Safety

More than one of these may apply to you. To gain clarity on which Life Lens you view the world through, take some time to journal about how these may fit (or not fit) into your life until you find the one that is the best fit.

7. FIND YOUR LIGHT
Spend time in self-discovery

How have you been avoiding doing the work?

....

....

And what will get you back on track when you find yourself doing this in the future? Make a checklist for yourself:

☐ 1. ....

☐ 2. ....

☐ 3. ....

☐ 4. ....

8. RADIATE YOUR LIGHT
Stop playing small

Create a vision board for how you may share your light with the world. Write or draw your ideas on this page.

9. THE MATRIX
How are you keeping yourself stuck?

what-if exercise

Think of three opportunities that you turned down in recent months. Write them out.

Opportunity:

....

Why you said no:

....

Emotion you felt at the time:

> Fear
>
> Anxiety
>
> Frustration
>
> Overwhelm
>
> Sadness
>
> Anger
>
> Exhaustion
>
> Guilt
>
> Shame
>
> Other:_____

What would have happened if you said yes instead:

....

....

....

....

....

....

....

Opportunity:

....

Why you said no:

....

Emotion you felt at the time:

Fear	*Anger*
Anxiety	*Exhaustion*
Frustration	*Guilt*
Overwhelm	*Shame*
Sadness	*Other:_____*

What would have happened if you said yes instead:

....

....

....

Opportunity:

....

Why you said no:

....

Emotion you felt at the time:

Fear	*Anger*
Anxiety	*Exhaustion*
Frustration	*Guilt*
Overwhelm	*Shame*
Sadness	*Other:_____*

What would have happened if you said yes instead:

....

....

....

10. YOUR SHADOW IS CALLING
Don't avoid the hard truths lying below the surface

Repeat the following three times per day for the next three days until it settles deeply within your mind, body, and energy:

> *I know that the path through
> my darkest shadows will lead me
> to my brightest light.*
>
> *I have faith in the plan that the
> Universe has for me, and trust
> that I do not need to know
> how things will unfold.*
>
> *I am always guided, fully held,
> and entirely safe.*
>
> *As I venture into my shadows,
> I know that the truth lying below
> the surface shall set me free.*

shadow work
GUIDEBOOK

DANIELLE MASSI, LMFT

STERLING ETHOS
New York

STERLING ETHOS
New York

STERLING ETHOS and the distinctive Sterling Ethos logo are registered trademarks of Sterling Publishing Co., Inc.

Text © 2025 Danielle Massi
Art © 2025 Union Square & Co., LLC

All rights reserved. No part of this publication may be reproduced, stored in a retrieval system, or transmitted in any form or by any means (including electronic, mechanical, photocopying, recording, or otherwise) without prior written permission from the publisher.

This publication is a component of *The Shadow Work Deck* (ISBN: 978-1-4549-6023-2) and is not to be sold separately.

For information about custom editions, special sales, and premium purchases, please contact specialsales@unionsquareandco.com.

Manufactured in China

2 4 6 8 10 9 7 5 3 1

unionsquareandco.com

Cover and interior design by Stacy Wakefield Forte
Cover and interior art by Inktally
Images on pages 18–20 by Hermine Blanquart/ The Noun Project

contents

WELCOME TO *THE SHADOW WORK DECK* . . .

Understanding Shadow Work 7
Working with *The Shadow Work Deck* 8
Card Spreads 10
About the Suits 16

THE CARDS

Shadow Facets 25
Energy Types 43
Jungian Archetypes 55
Shadow Astrology 61
Activation Cards 69

welcome to *the shadow work deck* ...

I'm thrilled you've decided to explore your own depths. Shadow work is a practice that requires a level of intimacy that can be challenging, but by engaging with it, you can gain insight that will help you live in alignment with every aspect of who you are, including the aspects of yourself that you may be avoiding or having difficulty accepting. *The Shadow Work Deck* is a tool on your path. These 40 cards highlight topics associated with shadow work, allowing you to apply their specific messages to your own life and enabling you to go deep within.

Shadow work is a practice that can be complemented by therapies like plant medicine and somatics, as well as these cards. The cards in this deck are intended as a tool to guide the exploration of your shadow by giving you specific areas to attend to. Rather than feeling lost and unsure of where to begin, the cards can focus your attention on specific areas of the shadow, answering the question, "Where do I even begin?"

This guidebook provides an overview of the cards, with in-depth explanations of the meaning behind each one, as well as information about shadow work and how to use this deck. The separate workbook is a great place for you to capture the thoughts that surface as you work with the cards. It also includes exercises to gently push you out of your comfort zone and help you consider the topics in the deck from a new perspective.

Many of the themes explored in this deck and corresponding workbook come directly from my work as a psychotherapist. In traditional talk therapy, the unconscious is difficult to tap into. But with tools like *The Shadow Work Deck,* you can access your unconscious mind and heal from burdens you have been carrying for far too long.

UNDERSTANDING SHADOW WORK

Carl Jung first coined the term *shadow* over a century ago when he was referring to the unconscious aspects of the self that individuals attempt to repress and bury. Although we all have a natural desire to hide unwanted characteristics within the deepest recesses of our minds, this can have a detrimental effect on our psyche if we continue to leave these unexamined.

Shadow work is the process of intentionally retrieving repressed information from the unconscious level of our minds in an effort to examine, integrate, and heal. Shadows cannot exist without the light, and the process of shadow work leaves individuals feeling relief, alignment, and peace as they allow the formerly unwanted aspects of self to integrate and make them feel whole. My sincere hope is that you use this deck as a tool to learn more about yourself as you navigate toward inner peace.

WORKING WITH *THE SHADOW WORK DECK*

Before you begin working with *The Shadow Work Deck,* create a clear and intentional atmosphere to minimize distractions and allow the information to flow more freely. Try to physically reduce the clutter around you, take a few deep breaths, and include any ritual tools that make you feel more in tune with your inner wisdom. Examples of ritual tools are shadow work–friendly crystals like howlite and black tourmaline, a lit candle, or burning incense. Whatever helps you feel more connected to your higher self, more able to access ease and clarity, allows for readings that will feel more intentional.

When your space is prepared and you are ready to use the deck, first set an intention for your reading. What is it that you are hoping to find out more about, or what pathways are you attempting to explore? Be clear, specific, and concise, and trust your gut about what questions you need answers to.

Here are some sample questions/intentions you can try thinking about:

What is holding me back in my life right now?

What have I been avoiding exploring?

Where can I focus my energy in order to see the most growth?

Once you have your question or intention in your mind, begin shuffling the cards while focusing solely on those thoughts. Feel your energy flowing out of your mind and heart, down your arms, and directly into the cards you are shuffling. Whenever you feel ready, stop shuffling.

Note: If any cards fall out of the deck during your shuffle, they are meant to be included in your card pull. Many spiritualists call these cards "jumpers" and believe they are very important messages for you to receive.

CARD SPREADS

When using this deck, you may find that you want to pull more than one card. This is what is known as a card spread or layout. These combinations can be used to gather even more information or gain deeper insight and clarity to the questions you are asking.

Here are some card spreads you can use with this deck:

PAST/PRESENT/FUTURE SPREAD

Pull three cards and place them in front of you face down.

PAST: The card on the left is a message about what you used to be/once faced.

PRESENT: The center card is what you are currently facing.

FUTURE: The card to your right is what you will face and/or what you need to know about your future.

DARKNESS AND LIGHT SPREAD

Pull two cards from the deck and place them in front of you in a stack.

DARKNESS: The card on the bottom represents the aspect of your shadow that is currently holding you back.

LIGHT: The card above it represents the area of yourself that you can draw strength (or light) from as you navigate through that shadow.

THE RELATIONSHIP SPREAD

Pull three cards and arrange them left to right.

The card on the left exemplifies the relationship issues you frequently encounter.

The card in the center shows you where improvement is needed to help your relationships thrive.

The card on the right illuminates where you have resistance to change in your relationships.

STREAM OF CONSCIOUSNESS SPREAD

This card pull will happen one card at a time. Shuffle your cards until you feel ready to stop, while setting an intention for a question you have. For example, you could ask, "How am I blocking my own success?" The card you pull after you ask that question will be your answer.

Use the answer to generate your next question, shuffling your cards and diving deeper with each response. For example, your next question could be, "What am I doing unconsciously to continue this cycle?" After asking your question, pull your next card.

Repeat this process up to five times.

SHADOW INTEGRATION SPREAD

Pull three cards from your deck and form them into a triangular shape.

THE TRIGGER: The first card, placed at the bottom left of your triangle, represents the way that your shadow is being projected into your life to let you know that an underlying shadow needs to be dealt with.

THE ROOT: The second card, placed directly to the right of the first card, exemplifies the underlying reason you are being triggered.

THE INTEGRATION: The third card, placed above and centered between the first two cards, illuminates the steps you could take to integrate the shadow so that it no longer triggers you.

ABOUT THE SUITS

There are five suits within *The Shadow Work Deck*, each representing a larger theme within the context of a shadow work journey. The suits are as follows:

SUIT 1: Shadow Facets (12 cards)
SUIT 2: Energy Types (8 cards)
SUIT 3: Jungian Archetypes (4 cards)
SUIT 4: Shadow Astrology (6 cards)
SUIT 5: Activation Cards (10 cards)

SHADOW FACETS

There are four facets of shadow work: Inner Child, Ancestral Healing, Past Life, and Womb Work. Each represents a specific type of shadow or unconscious memory that individuals are likely to repress within the psyche. The cards in this suit will offer insights into specific areas of your own shadow where information may need to be attended to.

ENERGY TYPES

The cards within the Energy Types suit directly correlate with your chakras, or energy centers. There are seven main chakras:

ROOT CHAKRA
(Muladhara)

LOCATION: Base of the spine
COLOR: Red
FUNCTION: Safety, security, grounding

SACRAL CHAKRA
(Svadhisthana)

LOCATION: Lower abdomen, behind the navel
COLOR: Orange
FUNCTION: Creativity, feminine energy, sensuality

SOLAR PLEXUS CHAKRA
(*Manipura*)

LOCATION: Center of the abdomen
COLOR: Yellow
FUNCTION: Personal power, masculine energy, confidence

HEART CHAKRA
(*Anahata*)

LOCATION: Center of the chest
COLOR: Green
FUNCTION: Love, compassion, openness

THROAT CHAKRA
(*Vishuddha*)

LOCATION: Throat
COLOR: Blue
FUNCTION: Communication, self-expression, truth

THIRD EYE CHAKRA
(Ajna)

Location: Forehead, between the eyebrows
Color: Indigo
Function: Intuition, insight, wisdom

CROWN CHAKRA
(Sahasrara)

Location: Top of the head
Color: Violet (or white)
Function: Spiritual connection, enlightenment, transcendence

The cards in this suit provide insight related to specific areas where energy is being blocked because of shadow, or unconscious memories.

JUNGIAN ARCHETYPES

Carl Jung introduced the concept of Jungian Archetypes to explain how we fall into innate, universal patterns as human beings. The archetypes are:

The Self	The Mother
The Shadow	The Father
The Anima/Animus	The Wise Old Man/Woman
The Persona	The Trickster
The Hero	The Child

The Jungian Archetype cards are an invitation to recognize areas for personal growth and potential integration. Some of these themes are addressed by other suits as well, which is why not all of these archetypes are included as their own individual cards within the deck. Inside, you will find cards specific to the Persona, the Mother, the Hero, and the Shadow.

SHADOW ASTROLOGY

Shadow Astrology is a unique look at darker or hidden aspects of the self that may be reflected in the astrological chart. This unique subset of astrology explores aspects of charts like the 12th House (where unconscious activities and self-sabotaging behaviors often lurk), planets like Pluto (which highlights challenges, transformations, and secrets), and aspects like Squares and Oppositions. The cards in the Shadow Astrology suit illuminate aspects of the self that need further exploration or integration based on struggles you may be facing within your own astrological chart.

ACTIVATION CARDS

The Activation Cards reveal a different aspect of self that is ready to be faced on your journey to self-actualization and enlightenment. These cards are catalysts for actions that you can take to shift yourself into a new paradigm of fulfillment and healing. Although the ideas presented on these cards may be triggering, those who listen and take action based on them will notice immediate differences in their energy, their relationships, and their lives. The cards in this suit are meant to do exactly as their title suggests: activate you to create positive change.

THE CARDS

shadow facets

Identify where your unconscious blocks are

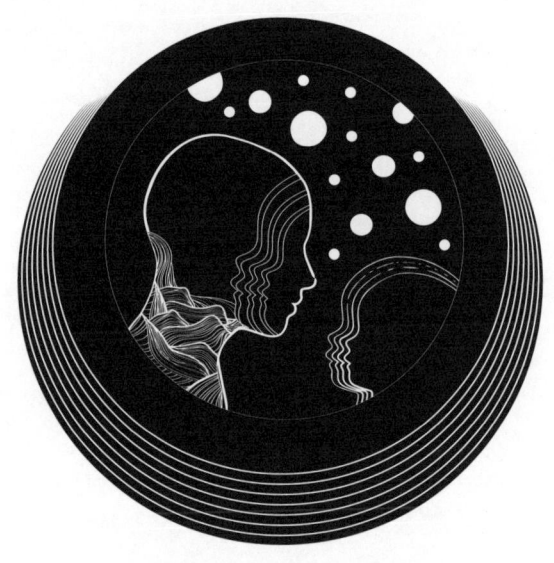

INNER CHILD

Heal your relationship with your younger self

SAFETY
Create boundaries and healing opportunities

Your inner child is the part of your psyche that holds onto the memories that have defined who you would grow up to become. Those experiences are in the past, but we can still create change and momentum by altering how those memories are stored within the mind, body, energy, and emotions.

Think back to a moment in your childhood that made a long-lasting impact on you because you needed a level of safety that wasn't there. Think about who should have been there protecting you, and why they might not have done so.

In this moment, how would you have responded differently if you were the adult in charge of your inner child's safety? And what would being protected that way have felt like in your body?

MANTRA

I release my attachment to the experiences my inner child faced in their past. My inner child is completely safe in my body and soul.

WONDER
Embrace freedom and play

All work and no play makes people burnt out and emotionally depleted, but hustle mindset is still alive and well within society. Although there is an abundance of research correlating stress and illness, stepping away from the need to be productive can be difficult.

This card invites you to infuse more fun into your life! Allow it to encourage you to see the world through the eyes of a child, with joy and excitement for the little things. Doing so will change your energy, and things will flow to you without having to use force. How can you let go of some rules and structure? And what are some specific things you can do today to have more fun?

MANTRA

Today I choose to embrace freedom and play, making decisions that light me up and bring me joy and levity.

OLD WOUNDS
Repeating themes from childhood

Our earliest memories create our perspective by forming pathways in the brain. These pathways create patterns, and one of these patterns is echoing in your present for a reason. This old wound now resurfaces as an opportunity for healing and growth. It has followed you from a specific instance in your childhood that lies unhealed, and breaking the cycle of reemergence will require you to shift how you handle this specific situation.

Begin by recognizing the theme that is showing up for you right now, then ponder when it has manifested in the past. When you experienced it before, how did you handle it? What can be done differently this time to break this pattern and stop it from ever showing up again?

MANTRA

I recognize the repeating themes from my childhood and how they have continually played out during my lifetime. This is the moment when I choose to respond differently, halting and eradicating the pattern for good.

ANCESTRAL HEALING

Remedy and release trauma

GENERATIONAL CURSES
Witness the patterns

Not all our shadows were created by us. Many of the traumas that we carry within ourselves have been passed down through our family's lineage, becoming our burden to carry. These generational curses can show up in the form of negative behaviors, psychological or physiological ailments, or persistent life challenges.

The Generational Curses card is presenting itself to you because there is a pattern to be witnessed within your family, but you have yet to formally acknowledge or attempt to heal it. This curse will persist until you make the decision to break it by excavating the shadow within.

MANTRA

I accept my role as the cycle breaker for myself, my ancestors, and the generations that will follow me. I bear witness to the curse my family bears, and I shine light upon it to release it for good.

LINEAGE
Reconnect with your ancestors

You are surrounded by the spirits of your ancestors as they attempt to connect with you and gently guide you through your life. They may try to bring awareness to their messages by showing you symbols that are intended to reassure you along your path. Your ancestors hold the wisdom of lifetimes, and their perspective can be an asset if you open yourself to receive their guidance.

Begin by closing your eyes, then take three deep breaths in the following pattern: breathe in through your nose for four counts, hold that breath for seven counts, then breathe out deeply. Repeat two times. Imagine your surroundings becoming cloudy as your ancestors emerge in your mind's eye. Let them give you guidance in whatever way you wish to receive it.

MANTRA

My ancestors are always with me, guiding me toward my highest and greatest good. I fully receive and accept their infinite wisdom.

REWRITE
Begin a new chapter

For so long, you have clung to a story that has shaped the way you perceive the world because of a narrative that has been passed through your family's generations down to you. But that old story is keeping you stuck in an outdated version of your own reality. This card is here to grant you permission to finally release your grip on the old narrative of your life that was handed to you by your elders, opting instead to rewrite it from the perspective of your most radiant future self.

Take a moment to think about the story your family has perpetuated that is currently blocking your ability to grow. What is the story, and how has it stopped you from making the best decisions for yourself throughout your life?

MANTRA

I no longer subscribe to the stories my family has told. I am the only author of my story, and I choose to empower myself by creating a new reality.

PAST LIVES
Travel back to create change

PAST LIFE
Own your gifts

Throughout our lifetimes, our souls are absorbing knowledge that we often forget as we are reborn into our next life. Although they may be consciously forgotten, these deeply rooted wisdoms are ever-present within our unconscious minds. Unlocking your access to your past lives opens the door to wisdom, experience, and gifts that will help you grow exponentially.

There is currently an opportunity for you to seize this knowledge from one of your past lives, and this card is a nudge for you to open the door to your past and accept this information. When you are ready, you will feel an immediate shift in your inner strength and wisdom as you accept that power into your spirit.

MANTRA

I choose to accept and embody the gifts that have been bestowed upon me from past versions of myself. As I integrate them, I feel their power and wisdom coursing through my entire energetic system.

SOUL JOURNEY
Discover where your soul has been

Your soul has experienced more lifetimes than you can fathom. While most of your hardships feel like they are happening for the first time, they are actually themes your soul has faced repeatedly. It is time for you to understand where your soul has been, and the lessons it has been tasked with learning. Doing so will rapidly shift your perspective, gifting you with the ability to understand that the low points you are experiencing are a gift rather than a curse.

Zoom out on your soul's experience. Shift your perspective to recognize that your current lifetime is a microscopic piece of your soul's journey. And this moment that is plaguing you is truly a blip on the radar compared with the vast expanse of where your soul has been.

MANTRA

I zoom out to remember the wisdom that comes with perspective. My shadows are pathways to the light.

PAST LIFE SCARS
Understanding hidden triggers

Right now a trigger shines a light on a pain point within your soul's past. This is not happening *to* you; it is happening *for* you. This discomfort is a window into your past, and an opportunity for you to address the underlying karmic loop that you have been playing out for lifetimes.

Close your eyes and ask yourself out loud, "What is the hidden trigger that my soul is asking me to recognize?" When the answer arrives, think about how that pain point has shown up in different areas of your life. Then close your eyes once more, and ask yourself, "What is this hidden trigger trying to show me about myself?" Allow that answer to settle deep within, illuminating not just the scar itself but also why it has been ever-present.

MANTRA

The scars of my past are beautiful opportunities for me to lean into my pain and allow it to teach me how to expand into a more radiant version of myself.

WOMB WORK

Integrate the shadow within your body

DIVINE FEMININE
Creativity, freedom, and flow

For too long, you have been out of balance with your feminine energy. By having either an excess of or a lack of feminine energy, you have been navigating your world from imbalance.

An excess of feminine energy can look like creation without action, codependency, mood swings, manipulation, jealousy, boundary issues, and lack of focus. It can physically manifest as reproductive problems, urinary tract infections, and addiction. A lack of feminine energy can look like a lack of creativity, sexual repression, disconnect or detachment, rigidity, or working too much. It can physically manifest as lower back pain, infertility issues, or bladder/kidney problems. Being in full alignment with your Divine Feminine requires balance between your masculine and feminine energies.

MANTRA

I awaken the flow of Divine Feminine energy within me, activating creation, freedom, and flow.

RELEASE
Relinquish your attachment to the trauma you carry

Without recognizing it, your traumas have become a part of who you are. Part security blanket, part armor, your attachment to your traumas has given you a false sense of safety by providing homeostasis but completely halting your growth. The hard truth is that you can't move on until you release your attachment to the trauma you carry.

Until you recognize how these traumas have served you, and actively choose to let them go, the weight of them will continue to keep you stuck. Examine the traumas that you cling to and take a deeper look at how they have served you until now. What benefits has your victimhood allowed you? And how has it halted your ability to evolve?

MANTRA

I thank my mind for trying to protect me by using my past to shield me. But I now choose to release so that I may be lighter and free, knowing that I am in total control of my destiny.

RELATIONSHIPS
Who are you holding onto that you shouldn't be?

Our relationships are mirrors of how we see ourselves, and through examining them we can deepen our understanding of the true nature of our feelings that we are repressing within the shadow. For example, when someone surrounds themselves with people who are dominating, they may be reflecting the shadow of a need to hide or to not be in control.

As we grow, however, the relationships may begin to feel dissonant and uncomfortable. This card is here to show you that there is a relationship in your life that you have outgrown but haven't yet let go of, and it may be time to reevaluate the place that relationship holds in your life.

MANTRA

I am ready to release any relationships in my life that are no longer aligned with where I know I am headed on my growth journey. I am grateful for the insight into my shadow that the relationship granted me, and I let it go freely and willingly as I step further into my power.

energy types

Align and balance your chakras

ROOT
Ground your energy

Think about gravity, the invisible but powerful force that is responsible for keeping our feet on the ground so that we don't float off into the ether. That unseen force that connects us to the Earth keeps us safe and centered. Although we don't reflect on it regularly, that rooted feeling makes it easier to make bold moves with the knowledge that we are grounded and secure.

At the base of our spine, our root chakra acts like a tether, and when in balance it grounds us and keeps us safe so that we can make decisions that will help us become more expansive.

This card is showing up for you because there is something in your life that is knocking you off-balance, messing with your center of gravity and causing you to react from a place of fear rather than responding from a place of centeredness and peace.

To get your root chakra back into alignment, spend some time grounding your energy. Try walking barefoot in the grass, doing some breath work in nature, and practicing a grounding mantra. All these things will help you release what is knocking you out of alignment, so that you have a balanced root chakra once again.

MANTRA

I am centered and grounded in the present moment. I release any fears or anxieties that are disconnecting me from the knowledge that I am rooted, protected, and strong.

CROWN
Connect with divine guidance and wisdom

Your crown chakra has been closed off due to memories that you have long buried away. While your mind works to hide those memories, your crown chakra remains closed, disconnecting you from divine guidance and wisdom. A closed crown chakra may physically manifest as headaches, trouble sleeping, confusion, lack of focus, and feeling like you are in a fog.

This is a sign to open your crown so that your spirit guides can channel messages to you. Doing so will also create balance within this energy center, bringing you peace and divine connection.

Imagine the fog within your mind clearing, like the sun emerging after a rainstorm. As you visualize this, breathe deeply, with your inhale bringing in the sun and your exhale clearing the fog of your mind.

MANTRA

I am a divinely connected, pure channel, and wisdom from my spirit guides finds its way to me with ease.

AJNA
Awaken your third eye

Your shadows can keep you stuck in cycles of dense emotions. Although necessary, these emotions need not be dwelled upon for too long. You may have pulled this card because these heavier emotions have blocked your innate intuitive abilities.

This card presents itself to those who have yet to fully realize the power of their psychic gifts. This is confirmation that you have abilities beyond what you imagine, and the only things standing in your way are fear and doubt.

If this is one of two cards you pulled, the other card is the area where your fear and doubt have originated from. Spend two to three minutes per day gently rubbing on your third eye (the space between your brow bones) as you recite the mantra below.

MANTRA

I release the fear and doubt that I have too long held onto, as I step into the next iteration of my abilities. I have psychic gifts beyond what I can imagine, and my third eye is awakening.

MANIPURA
Take control of your life

Your solar plexus, located in the center of your abdomen, is an area of your energy field that is holding onto shadow. Balance, self-esteem, and power are all controlled by this energy center, so if you have pulled this card, it means that yours is out of alignment.

Pulling this card means that you need to take control of your life in a way that feels natural and easy, without trying to force it (if your energy center is overworking) or retreat (if your energy center is underworking).

Take a moment to ponder how your solar plexus has been feeling and make a plan to dive into the shadow that has been knocking this energy center out of alignment, so that you may feel balanced once more.

MANTRA

I am confident and capable of standing in my power. I trust my decisions and know that my body and I are completely in sync as I navigate my world.

VISHUDDHA
Use your voice

Your voice matters, and you are not using it for something important. Biting your tongue is not serving you, nor is it serving those around you. Although using your voice here may be difficult, this issue needs to be brought to the light.

If this issue is a secret you are carrying for someone else, it may be time to tell them how this feels and urge them to change that. If it is an inequity that you have witnessed, you may be the person who can create change. And if it is something you have been longing to say, this is your sign to finally let it out into the open.

Think about how it will feel to unburden yourself of this information you are not voicing. Feel the release in your throat as you breathe deeply into that reality, finding the courage to say what has long needed to be said.

MANTRA

My voice is powerful, and my words will create a healing effect for myself and others that will vibrate throughout time.

ANAHATA
Where has your heart been closed off?

Throughout our lifetimes, accumulated heartbreaks can lead us to close our hearts. Drawing this card indicates that your heart center is closed off, and healing is necessary to reopen it.

Hold this card to your chest, close your eyes, and take several deep breaths. As you breathe, delve deep within and ask your heart to reveal where it has closed off. Bear witness to the moments that led to this closure, acknowledging the pain you have experienced. With each inhale, envision healing energy flooding into your heart, gently opening it. With each exhale, release past heartbreaks, allowing them to dissipate and leave your body.

Continue this process until you feel lightness in your heart. Know that healing is a journey, and that with each breath you are nurturing your heart back to wholeness.

MANTRA

I open my heart to the love and healing that I deserve.

SACRAL

Heal your connection to your sensuality

You are being called to heal your connection to not only the physical vessel that you are in, but also its innately sensual and beautiful nature. Your body is a temple, and the connection you have to it and the immense power that radiates from your sacral chakra will help you grow exponentially.

Identifying what may be halting the flow of energy in this chakra will break open the dam of your power, helping you feel in control of your emotions and free of your energetic burdens and shadows.

What is your connection to your sensuality? How do you feel in your naval center? And what shadow could potentially be slowing down your energy center? Ponder these questions as you work to heal your connection to your sensuality and your emotions.

MANTRA

I radiate sensual energy and power from my sacral chakra. I am empowered and free.

AURA
Become the master of your energy

Quantum physics shows us the connection between energy and matter—that all things are energy, including our physical forms. This perspective means that we can become the master of our energy by recognizing the unbridled power we have over ourselves.

To take it a step further, human beings also have control of the energy that is within their auras, or the subtle energy fields that exist around their physical forms, and can expand it with nothing more than their minds.

This card has appeared for you because you are far more powerful than you realize, and it is time for you to begin to work with your own energy to shift your life. You have done the inner work to lay the foundation for healing that is focused on expansion and frequency shifting, and can use that foundation as you begin to exist on a higher frequency.

To do so, begin incorporating aura expansion work into your daily practice by visualizing your aura and willing it to expand with nothing more than your thoughts and your breath. Remember the rule of quantum physics: everything is energy. Knowing this, let your visualizations begin to shift your reality as you step into your most powerful form.

MANTRA

Everything is energy, and I have complete control over my innate ability to amplify mine as I become exactly who I have always dreamed I would become.

jungian archetypes

Who are you at your core?

PERSONA
Recognize the different masks you wear

You have learned to carefully curate versions of yourself that you show the world. But hidden underneath it is your authentic expression. Who you are is worthy and wonderful, and that genuine self is getting lost underneath your masks, or personas. The Persona card is showing itself because you are losing yourself to your masks.

The personas we wear are bandages for larger issues. And the more you wear your masks, the less energy you give to your authentic nature. Peeling back your personas requires recognizing what they are and why you have created them. Spend some time exploring what yours may be, and why you may have begun wearing them. Then contemplate if you can release or integrate them.

MANTRA

I recognize the masks I wear, and while I understand the role they have had in protecting me, I choose whether or not they are still necessary. I am in total control of my personas.

HERO'S JOURNEY
Transformation and adventure

You are being called to begin a journey. The Hero archetype in Jungian psychology is often a willing participant eager to dive headlong into epic battles, but you may find yourself moving with more trepidation. It is time for you to search within yourself for courage and determination as you seek to venture into the unknown.

This card is urging you to move beyond what is familiar and into a journey that will make you uncomfortable, stretching your limits and expanding your possibilities. The knowledge you gain will help expand you and your capacity for self-love and growth.

MANTRA

I willingly embark on a Hero's Journey, leaving the comfort of the known behind as I forge my path. I am strong, resilient, and courageous, and I will use all the tools at my disposal to overcome any challenges I may face.

MOTHER
Nurturing and protection

You have been working tirelessly on yourself, but what you need most now is to refill your cup. Call upon the archetype of the Mother, and let her flow through you with nurturing, protection, and love.

How can you give yourself the loving care that you need? In what ways can you protect yourself during this retreat? By refocusing on your self-care, your emotions, and your needs, you will surround yourself with the love of the Mother. Tend to yourself now so that you may continue, replenished, your journey into the depths of your soul.

MANTRA

I wrap myself in the warm embrace of the Mother archetype as I choose to love myself fully, rest completely, and protect my energy as I nurture myself with all my heart.

SHADOW
What are you repressing?

When the Universe wants us to heal a shadow, it presents opportunities in the form of ordeals that must be faced. These trials may start small, but left unacknowledged they will become increasingly intense.

This card presents itself to those who have been practicing avoidance of a shadow that the Universe is steering them toward, whether in blissful ignorance or because of a deep fear of confronting the uncomfortable. You may have been catching glimpses of a specific, recurring issue in your life, but you haven't taken the time to address it. And now this shadow has been left unhealed for too long. Think about the obstacles you have faced and look for the common thread. What lies underneath is a shadow that is telling you it can no longer be ignored.

MANTRA

I willingly open myself to witness the shadows that the Universe has placed before me, and I am ready to heal them to the fullest extent possible.

shadow astrology

Let the stars be your guide

DARK MOON
Ending of a cycle. Opportunity for integration

The Dark Moon is a misunderstood and often overlooked phase when the moon receives no illumination. The Dark Moon is the final moment of the moon's cycle before it transitions to New Moon, a lingering pause before the cycle begins anew. Human beings often skip pauses and breaks, opting instead to keep pushing forward and moving on to whatever they believe is a productive next step. It's rare for people to slow down and allow themselves to simply be in the present, which is exactly what the Dark Moon beckons us to do.

The Dark Moon is an invitation to pause. By allowing time to rest and breathe, lessons can be integrated and embodied. Pauses are an essential and powerful part of growth.

MANTRA

I embrace the Dark Moon's invitation to pause and integrate. I am opening up to the myriad of possibilities that come from being present with my mind, body, and energy.

NEW MOON
Get clear on your intentions

The New Moon is the beginning of a cycle, where seeds are planted for future growth. This card is indicating that you should return to the beginning, and start with setting clear intentions around your shadow work goals. Take time to retreat from the world and embrace the quiet of nature and solitude.

In this space of stillness, think through your ultimate goals: Where do you wish to be at the end of your shadow work journey? How do you hope to feel when you get there? Knowing where you want the road to lead will help provide a clear path for its beginning. By embracing the beginning the New Moon provides, you will lay a solid foundation for the expansive healing work to come.

MANTRA

I open my heart to my new beginning and the healing my soul is ready for.

FULL MOON
Reap what you have sown

The Full Moon is the completion of a cycle. A culmination of the work that has been done, this phase is a full circle moment that illuminates all the effort you have put into your shadow work to uncover your depths and heal yourself.

While shadow work is a continual journey, take a moment to bask in the light that you have created for yourself. Allow the glow of the Full Moon to provide any additional insights and clarity into the inner work that you have done recently, connecting the final dots so that you may fully understand and integrate your shadows in the light of this moon. And if there are any lingering aspects that you have yet to completely release, this card is an invitation to explore them further so that you can move on to the next phase of your healing.

MANTRA

I bask in the light I have created for myself, allowing it to illuminate all parts of me until I am whole.

CHIRON
Transmute your pain into power

Chiron, known as the wounded healer, holds the key to our greatest transformations. Chiron's influence brings to light wounds that run deep, such as karmic cycles, ancestral traumas, or early childhood experiences that have haunted us. If this card appears for you now, it signals a profound pain yearning to be transmuted.

When this card appears alongside a card from Shadow Facets, it indicates the specific type of trauma Chiron is illuminating. Similarly, when paired with a card from Energy Types, it points to the energy center or chakra where the trauma resides.

This card may also symbolize that you are meant to work as a guide, teacher, or healer, using the transmutation of your pain into power to help others do the same.

MANTRA

I am finally ready to transmute the deep pain I have been carrying into blazing light that I may use to illuminate the paths of those who follow me.

BLACK MOON LILITH
Harness your power

Black Moon Lilith is a powerful concept in shadow astrology associated with the repressed needs around power and sensuality. It represents the primal aspects of the self that are raw and untamed, which can manifest in self-destructive ways. However, when this power is harnessed positively, it can become our greatest asset.

This card is a powerful urging to tap into your true, unfiltered, primal nature. It may indicate that it is time to diverge from the path others expect you to follow. This could involve reclaiming aspects of your femininity and sensuality that have been suppressed. Although this choice may unsettle those around you, let it empower you to recognize the true strength that has always existed within. The transition heralded by Black Moon Lilith can be extremely powerful for those who embrace it fully and completely.

MANTRA

I embrace my deepest desires, and embrace every aspect of who I am. I am free.

MERCURY RETROGRADE
Learn to communicate

There is currently a breakdown in your communication style that is making it difficult for people to understand you. If this issue is recurrent, explore the moments throughout your life where you have noticed this happening. If this is the first time, why may this situation be occurring right now, and how can you get your communication back on track?

If you pulled this card with the Vishuddha card, spend extra time attending to your throat chakra. Consider drinking warm tea, ingesting a spoonful of honey, and wearing a blue scarf or crystal necklace to protect the area until your communication breakdowns cease. You may also consider adding chanting or singing into your meditation routine to activate the throat and help create balance and alignment.

MANTRA

I am clear about my desires and communicate them with ease. I speak my truth with clarity and compassion.

activation cards

Create change through action

EGO
Overcoming your inner critic

Your inner critic has been influencing your decision-making. Although that ego voice is a protective mechanism of the brain, it isn't necessarily acting in your best interest. It is time to put a new voice in the driver's seat: your intuition.

Forcing the ego to take a back seat requires a bit of shadow work. If you pulled this card with another, look to the secondary card to uncover where the voice of your inner critic originated. Once you know where this voice initially developed, you can work to reduce or even eliminate the hold that it has on you.

MANTRA

I know my ego is trying to protect me, but I trust my intuition to take control of my decision-making and know that everything will work out for my highest and greatest good.

KARMIC LOOP
Break the chain

The path that you must choose to walk will be a disruptor for your lineage. This path will not be easy, but walk it anyway. The ripple effects may create friction within your family. Choose this anyway. Your role in unburdening your lineage from the karmic loop that they are engaged in isn't fair. Do it anyway. You are the cycle breaker, and the Universe is guiding you to this moment for a reason.

Karmic loops are repeated patterns that soul groups experience lifetime after lifetime until one brave soul breaks the chain. That responsibility falls to you now, and the Universe will hold you every step of the way.

MANTRA

I accept the role of the cycle breaker for my lineage. Every breath I take imbues my body with courage to navigate this duty and break the chain permanently.

SACRED RAGE
Unleash your anger to amplify your power

Although anger is often seen as a lower vibrational emotion, it can be harnessed and channeled intentionally. Sacred rage involves reclaiming your power and voice, transforming pain into undiluted energy and strength.

This card appears to you because the injustices you face have become burdens that you carry, and your body is urging you to release them.

Your sacred rage can be expressed through rituals such as dancing, screaming, writing your anger onto paper and burning it, or any other method that helps you transmute this deep-seated emotion from your body. Embrace this process and allow your sacred rage to become a source of empowerment and transformation.

MANTRA

I honor my sacred rage and reclaim my power. Through intentional release, I transmute my pain into strength and energy. I trust in the healing power of my darkest emotions and embrace my journey toward empowerment and growth.

STARSEED
Connect with galactic groups

You are divinely influenced by spirit guides, and that includes beings from galactic groups. If you pulled this card, it means that your galactic guides want to work with you, directing you along on your journey and aiding as you take pivotal steps on your path. It also is confirmation that your soul originated from another planet, star system, or galaxy.

Your soul is ancient, and the connection that you have with these guides will reveal a new depth of inner wisdom. Embrace all that comes with this.

Allow yourself to visualize a beam of light extending out of your crown, through the sky, and up into space. Let that beam of light find its way to the galactic group that is looking to work with you, and allow their wisdom to drop in.

MANTRA

I am a Starseed on Earth. I honor my galactic ancestors and their wisdom. Through love and light, I awaken my true purpose. I am connected, I am guided, I am one with the Universe.

DARK GODDESS
Embrace the darker path: intuition, mystery, and magic

The Dark Goddess is calling to you. She is holding you through your deepest pain, guiding you through your biggest fears, and offering wisdom as you find yourself trapped at your rock bottom.

If you have pulled this card, you may be currently experiencing or are about to experience a profound low point. Look to the Dark Goddess to walk you through this moment, and lean into the darker path rather than retreating from it. If you grant her the ability to lead the way, this moment can imbue you with your greatest strength.

Opening yourself to the wisdom that your darkness can offer will heighten your intuitive gifts and create rifts that allow magic to shine through the dark. Let the Dark Goddess guide you, and feel a deep internal shift as you give her the reins.

MANTRA

I am not afraid because I am divinely guided by the magic and wisdom of the Dark Goddess. I trust that this is happening for me, not to me, and my deepest lows will elevate me to my greatest highs.

LIFE LENS
Understand how you see the world

Your Life Lens is the perspective you see the world through based on your early life experiences. These moments have shaped your mind to view the world in a unique way, and they can be summed up into the following categories:

- Freedom
- Control
- Fairness
- Power
- Safety

The Life Lens card is an indicator that whatever struggle you are currently going through is being influenced by the particular perspective through which you see the world. Understanding exactly how your Life Lens is impacting your struggle will help you start to untangle the chokehold this shadow has on you.

MANTRA

I accept that my Life Lens has impacted my view, and I am ready to shift my perspective based on powerful and supportive experiences.

INNER LIGHT
Spend time in self-discovery

You have been avoiding digging deeper into your soul's truth for some time now, allowing yourself to get caught up in surface-level healing or putting off the inner work in lieu of responsibilities or productivity. That avoidance must come to an end.

This card is an indicator that there is deeper inner work to be done to fully uncover who you are and what you are meant to do in this world. Going into the depths of your own soul will aid you in stepping into your true purpose. Take some time and truly dig deeper on your journey of self-discovery. Trust your path and find your light.

MANTRA

I am ready to go deep within to uncover the truth about myself and find the light within.

RADIANCE
Stop playing small

The time for hiding your gifts, talents, and wisdom is coming to an end. Until now you have smothered your own light for the comfort of others, but that is not serving them and it is certainly not serving you.

From this point, it is your responsibility to radiate the light that you have cultivated out into the world. Do not worry about the opinions of others or concern yourself with what-if scenarios, as those are only stopping you from reaching your own potential. If this card has revealed itself to you, you need to boldly step into the spotlight in every way, shape, and form that feels aligned for you.

MANTRA

I will no longer hide my gifts, shy away from the spotlight, or make myself small to create comfort for others. I will proudly radiate my light for the world to see.

MATRIX
How are you keeping yourself stuck?

Your brain is designed to keep you in predictable routines, ensuring your safety but halting your growth. Without recognizing it, your mind has been working to stop you from pursuing opportunities that would propel you closer to the goals that you have been working tirelessly to accomplish.

Recognize the prospects that have been put in front of you lately that you ultimately declined. If you would have bravely and courageously said yes to any one of them, how might things be different right now? On its way is a new opportunity for you to break free from the matrix of your mind. Recognize the fear that comes with the prospect as the brain attempts to keep you in the predictable known, and remember that the feeling is not an indicator of how saying yes to this will play out.

MANTRA

I thank my mind for trying to keep me safe, but I am ready, willing, and able to take control of my own destiny and break free of the matrix of my mind.

THE CALLING
Don't avoid the hard truths lying below the surface

You are being called to trust the path the Universe is laying out for you. The road you begin to walk may feel frightening at times because it is full of harsh realities and hard work, yet this path will grant you the freedom you so deeply crave.

Don't avoid your shadows. Let your heart lead the way. Trust that the Universe has set you on this path because you are ready to face your shadows head on, and there is nothing to be afraid of besides this truth: your life will feel wildly different when you are done. Your journey into your shadow likely won't look the way you anticipated, but have a little faith that it will be everything that you need and so much more. You are ready for this. Your shadow is calling.

MANTRA

I trust in the path the Universe is laying out for me, and I willingly face my darkness with the knowledge that going into the dark will lead me to my illustrious light.

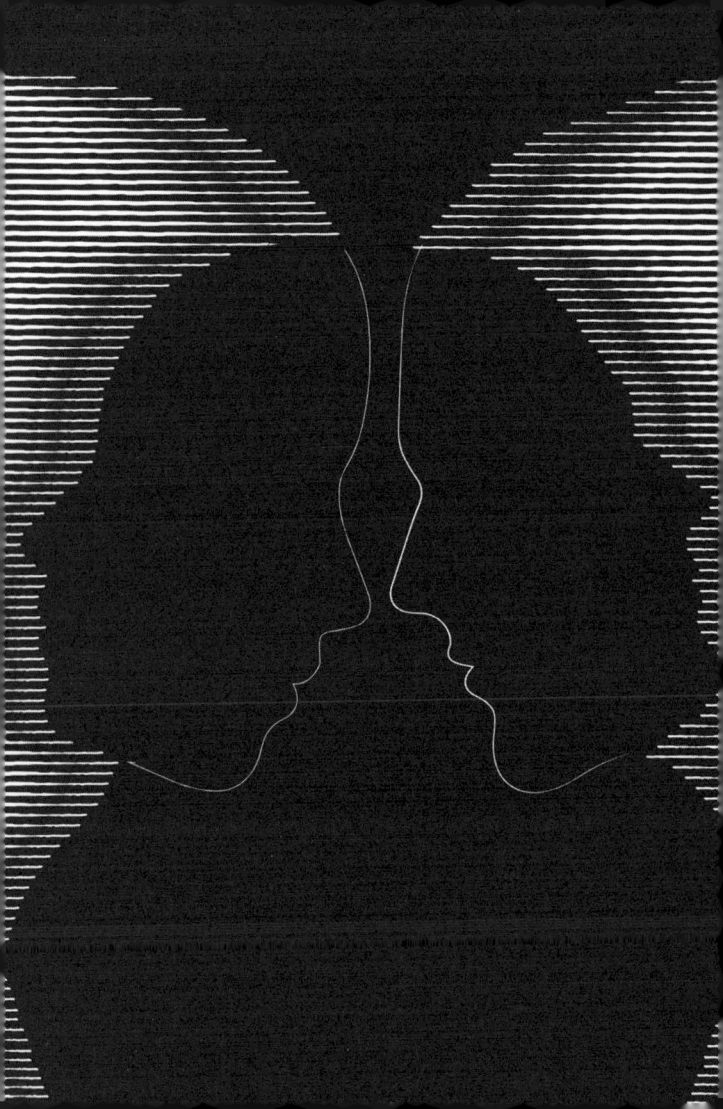